TEACH YOUR KIDS
ABOUT
MONEY

A guide to teaching your kids
about money and finance over the ages

NINA PAGE

TABLE OF CONTENTS

INTRODUCTION

AS THE OLD SAYING GOES, MONEY MAKES THE WORLD GO ROUND! And it's definitely essential in all of our lives. We need it to buy food, pay our household bills, go on vacation, you name it, money is involved. So, without it, we wouldn't be able to do very much.

Some people would describe themselves as being terrible with money. That might mean that they spend everything they have and have nothing left by the end of the month, or they might just mean that they're super disorganized and don't know how much money they've got or how much they need. Others, like me, are incredibly organized, have spreadsheets coming out of their ears and know precisely what they have to the exact cent. Can you resonate with any of these?

There is some research to suggest that the way we think about and relate to money as an adult stems from what we were taught growing up, what we heard, or how we saw others act around money. For example, a study by The University of Cambridge found that money habits are already ingrained by the time we reach the age of seven.

So as a parent, remember those little eyes are watching and listening to everything you do. If you and your partner are arguing about money, they'll notice. If you slap down the plastic at every buying opportunity, they'll notice that too. So try and set good examples.

I remember when I was a kid, my mum would say that we didn't have any money; my dad was awful at managing his money and still is to this day, but he was very generous. Can you remember how your parents were with money? Have you picked up any of their habits? What good money habits can you trace back to your childhood? Or what bad habits do you think have come from your time as a child? If it helps, write it all down.

Every parent wants the best for their kids - whether that be the latest gadgets, the best education, or a good group of friends. And we all know that without a good knowledge of how money works, it can be extremely difficult to do well in life, which is why most parents also want to be able to teach their kids about money. It will equip them with the knowledge and skills needed to manage their money effectively as they move into adult life and have to fend for themselves.

Many parents share the same concerns when it comes to their childrens' money skills and being able to pass on the best money skills to their kids. Yet many parents aren't helping their kids become financially literate. T. Rowe Price's '11th Annual Parents, Kids & Money' Survey found that almost half of all parents missed opportunities to teach their kids about money and managing finances and a staggering 25% were afraid to even talk to their kids about the subject of money. The kids who took part in the survey actually wanted their parents to teach them more about money!

Many parents want to know when the best time is to start talking to their kids about money or how they teach them the value of money. They want to know how to convince their youngsters that going to college will be worth it in the long-term.

Are these some of the concerns you can resonate with? Well, you've come to the right place. This book will go into how you can help your kids learn about money and the right skills they need. I'll also go into some detail on what you can be teaching your kids at different ages.

In fact, it can be easy to teach your kids about money by turning day-to-day activities into learning activities. What kid doesn't like to have fun, even if they're learning at the same time? So, I'll be suggesting plenty of ways that you can do this, too.

If you want to play a vital role in shaping your children's feelings, thinking and values about money, you need to give them the gift of financial literacy from an early age. This book tells you how!

THE RULES FOR TALKING TO YOUR KIDS ABOUT MONEY

I'M NOT SURE I REALLY LIKE THE WORD 'RULES.' I PREFER 'play,' and we'll get on to that later. But the rules don't apply to your kids - they apply to you. So, unless you exercise some discipline in the way you talk to (and in front of) your kids when you're talking about money, they're going to get mixed messages.

So okay, these are the rules.

RULE NUMBER 1: START TALKING TO YOUR KIDS ABOUT THE BASICS FROM A YOUNG AGE

Research shows that by age three, kids are already starting to form money habits and learn more about how money works, and by age seven, they have pretty much formed their money habits and attitudes that will take them into adult life. Yet many parents don't have 'the money conversation' until their children are older.

Even before they can say very much, kids will see you using money in everyday life, from buying groceries to buying them toys from the toy store. It is good for them to see you make purchases with cash. Once they can talk, tell them what you're doing when you go to the shops. Explain that you're using money or your card to buy things. Show them the receipts; repeat this every time you purchase something. They will soon learn what money is and what it is used for.

Having conversations about money helps to build their confidence on the subject and helps to develop their financial management skills. It has been found that the children that have conversations about money when growing up are the ones who manage their money better once they grow up.

Make it fun; we all know that learning is easier when we're having fun. So, if you're stuck with what to do in the school holidays or at weekend, do some activities that involve learning about money. Gentle lessons in money can educate your kids while also having fun at the same time.

RULE NUMBER 2: TALK TO YOUR KIDS ABOUT DIGITAL MONEY

Remember that money now includes virtual money, so you need to also show your kids how to use digital money. Credit and debit cards have been around a long time now, but other forms of money also play a major part in all of our lives. Let them watch your balance fall on the card machine when withdrawing cash from the bank. Repeat this over and over with different examples.

As many adults have learned, the problem with credit cards is that by breaking the immediate link between cash and what you can spend, they seem like a magically inexhaustible fund of money. But, unfortunately, they're not. So, what you need to explain to your kids is how your cards link to your bank account. Showing how the balance falls at the ATM is a great way to do this.

Most kids nowadays have mobile phones from a young age. For the youngest kids, use a top-up card so that they learn when it runs out, they have to wait until the next month to be able to use it again. For an older child, you may want to use a contract phone that blocks any of the activities you have not included in the monthly fees to learn they can't just spend money without thinking about it.

RULE NUMBER 3: INSTILL INTO YOUR KIDS THE IMPORTANCE OF SAVING

We all have at least one friend who is terrible at saving. They never have money to pay for a last-minute vacation or are always complaining that they have nothing left at the end of every month. It would be interesting to know if they were ever taught how to save when they were growing up.

With young kids, their first experience with money will likely be spending, as they watch you buy things for them and the family. But we also need to teach them the flip side to spending and that is how to save money. Teaching kids to save is useful in so many different ways. Not only will it instill into them the habit of saving, which will benefit them in later life, it also teaches them how to be appreciative of money, it teaches them discipline of not spending all their money and it teaches them the benefits of delayed gratification. It can also teach them organization and planning skills because by saving, they may plan how to use that money in the future. Finally, it helps them see how they can build security and independence. As you can see, there are so many valuable lessons learned when our kids learn the value of saving!

Like most parents, you probably give your kids pocket money once they get old enough, or if you still have a young child, this is something that you have already thought about.

Getting them a piggy bank or even a glass jar will do. Every time you give them pocket money, encourage them to keep an amount of it aside to 'save.' You could even encourage them to have two separate piggy banks; one for spending and one for saving. That way, they can learn the difference between spending and saving.

Use positive words when encouraging them to save; tell them, *"I love to save," "saving is such a great habit."*

If you are teaching your kids the benefit of saving from a young age, you can always encourage them by keeping it short-term. For example, they may have had their eye on a particular toy that all the kids have. Encourage them to save up for it and let them know how many weeks it will take to save enough money to buy it. You can teach them more long-term saving skills once they get a little older and understand the concept a bit more. If you teach them about short-term goals, this should easily then progress into long-term habits as they get older.

You could even go a step further by matching what they save. Greenlight or FamZoo are prepaid debit cards and apps that allow parents to transfer their kids money and pay interest, which of course, encourages saving.

RULE NUMBER 4: GIVE YOUR KIDS OPPORTUNITIES TO EARN MONEY

To learn how to manage money and make decisions with money, kids need to have their own money. Many parents will start giving their kids an allowance from a certain age, or 'pocket money' as some may know it by.

One of the best ways kids can learn the value of money is if they have to earn it. So instead of just handing your kids an allowance every week, why not make them earn it first? One of the best ways to do this is by giving them chores to do around the house. Washing the dishes or cleaning their room are great ways for them to earn their allowance. Everyone appreciates the money they have earned a lot more than the money they have been given.

However, be careful not to get into a situation where you are paying your kids for each and every chore they do around the house. They also need to learn that helping out doesn't always mean they get paid; it's part of family life. So, the allowance should be payment for certain chores only; make it fun and decide together with your kids.

One fun way to pay an allowance is to pay them an amount equal to their age. So, if they're seven years old, pay them $7 a week/month or £7. Or work out what you spend on them in a particular area, such as social activities in a year, divide it by twelve and give this to them as a monthly allowance. Then, increase it over time to include other areas such as buying clothes. This will increase their confidence over time and let them see that you trust them. But you may decide that just because they're a year older, this shouldn't mean they also get a higher allowance.

An alternative to starting to pay an allowance with your younger kids is to pay them a 'special allowance,' which is a fixed sum to spend at a specific event such as a football game or a party. It will feel like something special, and you can use it as an opportunity to let them spend it as they wish and provide them with guidance on what things cost and let them see the different options of things they can buy. Make sure that they know that once the allowance has been spent, it's gone and they won't get any more (and here's a significant rule for you - when you say, "you won't get any more," stick to that decision. Money lessons have to be learned, and some kids will need to learn them the hard way).

If you have chosen the right amount to pay your kids, there will be times when they run out partway through the week or month. It's important in these situations not to bail them out by giving them more money. But it's also important to ask why they ran out of money. Did they lose a pound coin, lend money to another child, have their money stolen, or just spend too much on sweets? Explore their choices with them and ask how they feel about the decisions they made.

You may decide to decrease the frequency of the allowance as they get older. For example, if you pay it weekly when they're younger, change it to every fortnight or monthly so that they can learn how to budget for a longer period of time, which they will need to do when they have a paid job. With teenagers, you may decide to stop the allowance in the summer months to encourage them to get a part-time job to earn money.

There is a fun app called GoHenry in the UK and US, which you can use to pay your kids an allowance. It's an excellent way for them to learn money management. The app lets you and your kids arrange a pocket money transfer, set savings goals, list chores, and give them extra ways to earn money. Greenlight and Famzoo also do a similar thing in the US (using an app will also help introduce kids to digital money, which is really helpful).

Giving your child an allowance also helps them to see that you have confidence in them by letting them 'have a go' with money. Talk to them about how they feel when they get an allowance and ask them what they're going to spend it on.

RULE NUMBER 5: HELP YOUR KIDS MAKE SMART SPENDING DECISIONS

Giving your kids an allowance is a great way for them to learn key lessons in money management. However, suppose you just give in to them and give them money whenever they want. In that case, they will never learn the value of money or how to live within a budget, which is crucial for when they eventually fly the nest and live in the real world of having to fund everything themselves.

To encourage money management, you could give them different jars; one for spending, one for saving and one for giving. But let them decide how much goes in each jar every month. You can talk through their decisions, and you should - you're helping them to learn the process of thinking through financial choices. Try to lead them, but in the end, the decision is theirs.

You also need to teach your kids that not all the money they use for spending is for things they want, but some money has to go on things they need. For example, in some households, the kids only ever buy toys and candy - they're not responsible for any of the day-to-day costs of their lives.

But in adult life, a lot of our money will go on necessities such as cleaning products for the house or gas for the car. So take the kids to the gas station, for instance, and show them how much it costs to fill the car. Show them your bills for local taxes, food, and so on.

They also need to realize that if they don't do certain things, it will cost them and they will need to pay someone to do these things for them. A good example of this is cleaning the house. If they don't do this, they will need to pay someone to help. You can teach this lesson to your kids by giving them chores to do and if they don't want to do them, it will cost them in part of their allowance. This is because they're effectively paying you to do the chores for them. But as kids get older, you can also ask them to find out how much an hour people earn for cleaning - look at cards in the window of a temporary employment agency, look at classifieds in the paper, or go on the web to search job listings.

When your kids are saving, regularly count the money they've saved with them. This will encourage them to save even more!

RULE NUMBER 6: TEACH THEM THE IMPORTANCE OF GIVING

One important lesson we all need to learn is the gift of giving. It is important to teach your kids from a young age the value they can give to others by giving away part of their money to help others who are less fortunate or others who are in need.

As we touched on earlier, a great way to do this is to give your kids a separate jar where they can allocate part of their allowance for giving.

You might show your kids some of the groups or causes you donate money to or open up opportunities for them by discussing the different groups and organizations that exist. For example, Greenlight and Famzoo will let your kids set up accounts for giving. If you set up an account with Kiva, which makes micro-loans to grassroots projects, you can discuss your choices together and when the children are old enough to talk about lending, you can see your repayments come in too.

Or you could encourage them to buy one thing for a local food bank next time you do a weekly shop. That's great for younger kids if the supermarket has a collection basket, as they can proudly put their own offering into the basket and feel proud of themselves.

www.charitynavigator.org is a great resource to find the right giving opportunities for your kids.

RULE NUMBER 7: TEACH YOUR KIDS THAT MONEY CAN GROW IN VALUE

Many of us contribute into pension pots as an adult and that money is invested into various funds so that hopefully our pension pot grows in value and gives us a good return on investment by the time we want to draw the pension down. So, for example, we might invest in the stock market or in real estate.

Saving is a great habit, but another valuable lesson we can teach our kids from a young age is the value of investing some of their money to increase its value and grow at a faster rate than their savings. It's like teaching your children that planting seeds is great, but you have to water the seeds for them to grow.

This may be a difficult concept for them to grasp when they're young, but as they get older, it should hopefully become easier to understand and you can open a custodial investment account on their behalf so that can see for themselves how their money can grow by investing it. Greenlight also now offers the opportunity for your kids to invest.

Get them a book they can read to learn about it; there are many of them out there for kids.

RULE NUMBER 8: SHOW YOUR KIDS WHAT GOOD FINANCIAL BEHAVIOR LOOKS LIKE

From a very young age, your kids will watch you with money every day, whether that be in the grocery store or the way you talk about money with your partner, friends, and family.

Research has shown that how we see our parents act around money or talk around money can shape our habits as an adult. It is therefore important that you model the right behaviors about money to shape the future behaviors of your kids.

Don't send your kids mixed messages. For example, saying you don't have any money and then taking them to the toy shop to buy a new toy sends mixed messages.

Don't be shy about talking to your kids about money and discussing with them the different values they need to learn about money. Trying to hide talking about anything related to money could give your kids the message that money is something that shouldn't be spoken about; being open and honest is the best way to teach them the values of money.

(Some people grow up feeling that money is somehow dirty or shameful because their parents refused to talk about it. As a result, they can often be very successful people in their careers but don't know how to handle their wealth. Money 'trouble' isn't just when the money runs out - it's when you have a bad relationship with it. Don't let your kids get like that).

If you want to teach your kids good spending and saving habits and good money management, show them what good looks like. Practice what you preach. And be consistent and clear in your messages to instill the good habits into them, which they can then take with them into adulthood.

RULE NUMBER 9: KEEP IT AGE-APPROPRIATE

Telling the truth about your own money situation is always a good idea, but you need to remember how much your kids can take on board depending on their ages.

Kids of different ages will understand different things. For example, if you're struggling one month and need to eat at home one weekend rather than eating out (if that's what you'd typically do), you can explain to younger children that you're going to eat at home because it costs less and that sometimes we have to make choices and sacrifice certain things we enjoy. You don't need to go into masses of detail; keep it short and sweet.

But if you're talking with a teenager, you might go into more detail about a couple of unexpected expenses (maybe a car repair and having to buy a new washing machine) or that the gas price has gone up and that hits the family budget.

RULE NUMBER 10: REMEMBER THEY KNOW MORE THAN YOU THINK!

Money is a bit like sex. You think your kids don't know very much, but you'd be surprised at what they have picked up from you, their friends, and the world around them. However, they may have missed out on a couple of important facts, they may have got a few things wrong, and they may also be confused about how it all fits together.

Most kids are pretty smart and what you think you've hidden from them, they've probably worked out for themselves. If you're rich and think you've hidden it from your kids, for instance, they will have figured it out from the house you live in and the lifestyle you lead, comparing to their friends or things they see on the TV or in magazines.

When they're growing up, they're naturally curious and may go about searching for things about you. The internet is a great tool for them to do a bit of spying on their parents. But kids lack context, especially younger kids. They often don't have things to compare to or are too inexperienced to have any context. They often lack the full picture and therefore, the price of something may not mean very much to them until they gain experience as they grow up and see the cost of more and more things. So they may know the prices of many things but not the actual value.

For instance, I knew exactly how much film stars got paid for each movie when I was a young teenager. I also knew the cost/value equation for every lipstick brand available in our local store. But I didn't know how much it cost to buy a house in our neighborhood, and I didn't realize that you had you pay tax!

RULE NUMBER 11: THINK BEFORE YOU TALK

Before you start talking to your kids about money, examine your own values. It's one thing to want your kids to learn that "money can't buy happiness", but if all you care about is the latest fast car or gadget, what will these teach your kids? They will quickly come to see that your fundamental values do not align with what you're telling them every day. Kids are definitely hard to fool. They'll catch you out quicker than you can say "piggy bank." Do this for too long and your credibility may be damaged forever. They may then never believe anything you tell them.

So it's vital that you make sure your values are aligned with what you teach your kids. And if you're in a couple, make sure your values are aligned with each other before you pass those onto your kids. For example, if, as parents, you follow different values about money, your kids will easily spot this and start exploiting this. This means you also need to be aligned on how you spend your money on your kids. Make sure you both agree on how you will spend money on clothes, toys, and other things. For older kids, this may start to include things like college and their first car.

If you want to teach your kids about the importance of giving back but never practice this yourself, they may become to doubt your words, no matter how often you deliver the message. Many kids look up to their parents to model themselves, especially when they're young; they act like sponges soaking everything up around them. You therefore need to walk the talk and practice what you preach, as just words often won't be enough.

If your family is non-conventional because you have divorced or there are stepkids, this may be more challenging because there could be more than one household, each with different values about money. The important thing here is to make sure your kids understand why you have chosen your values.

RULE NUMBER 12: DON'T BE ASHAMED TO TALK ABOUT MONEY

For many households, the subject of money can bring up feelings of guilt or embarrassment. Maybe you feel like you haven't been as successful as you wanted to be. If you're wealthy, you may feel like you need to shelter this from your kids so as not to crush their drive and ambition to succeed at something. But look at it this way; you can use the fact that you're wealthy to educate your kids about what wealth means and talk to them about the challenges and responsibilities that come with having lots of money. For example, why do we value money so much? How did we accumulate it and what were the challenges along the way? How would we feel if we lost it and how would we deal with it?

Or perhaps you chose to follow a career in social enterprise, or let's say, decided to be a lawyer working on human rights cases rather than making big bucks working for corporations. So, you have less money than the families of some of your kids' friends, but you're glad you chose the path you did.

Discuss these things openly with your kids and let them see your money values. Don't be afraid to have these conversations.

RULE NUMBER 13: TALK WITH THEM, NOT AT THEM

Teaching your kids about money is not an opportunity to lecture them about the differences between right and wrong. Kids will respond much better and more openly if you actually discuss things with them, ask them questions, let them tell you what they think. If you can get them to engage, they are much more likely to take in what you're trying to teach them.

Empathy is important. For instance, if you can't afford something a child wants, don't just say "no." Say, "I understand how much you want that, but right now, we can't afford it." You might suggest they can save up for it, or even that if they can save half the money, you'll make up the rest - but try to understand their feelings (what did you most want when you were that age? Do you remember?).

Games are a great way to get your point across and can be used from a young age. However, be mindful of not being dismissive of your kids' views or belittling them. Avoid using phrases such as "when you're old enough to understand" or "maybe when you're older" - just tell them as much as they can understand at their age.

If you are having a conversation about money when they're around, ensure you involve them in the discussion or bring it down to their level to make it easy for them to understand what is being discussed. This will vary according to age or level of maturity.

A great way to help them learn is for you to challenge them, ask them questions about their money beliefs, get them thinking about them. For example, why do they have certain beliefs? What have they heard other people say about money?

RULE NUMBER 14: QUESTIONS, QUESTIONS, QUESTIONS

We have already mentioned this, but asking questions is a great way to get your kids to engage and get them thinking about money and what it means to them. Ask them if they believe you are rich or poor. What makes them think that? Ask them about celebrities and people in the public eye. Who do they think is rich? How do they think they achieved it? Ask them what it means to be rich; this is a great question to get them thinking about money.

Sometimes, celebrities go bankrupt because they can't control their spending impulses. What do your kids think about that? Do they think they could cope better? How would they manage things?

Ask them what they would do if they had $20 million. Would they be happier? How would it change their life? Does being rich make people happy or sad? And flip it; ask them why they think some people are poor. Are they happy?

You will want to keep repeating these questions at different ages. Has their opinion changed? Have they learned anything new as they get older?

Please make sure you also give your views on each question and explain that being rich means different things and that people get their happiness in different ways.

RULE NUMBER 15: CHOOSE YOUR WORDS CAREFULLY

It is important that the things kids hear about money are the right things, especially at a young age when what you say can make a bigger impression on them. If kids hear something like "I'm glad I don't need to drive a car like that" or "He looks like he made those clothes himself," this can lead young ears to associate money with happiness and that is definitely not something you want them to think going into adulthood.

Suppose you are fortunate enough to have money, while it is sensible to let kids know that discussions about the family's wealth are between family members only. You should not encourage them to keep the wealth a secret in public as this can foster unhealthy relationships about wealth and can lead to dangerous situations with money as an adult. Never make them feel like money is something that should be kept a secret or something that they can't discuss with friends.

RULE NUMBER 16: INVEST IN YOUR KIDS

You may be a low earner or a middle earner, or you may have gone from nothing and through your passion for your work, hard work and determination, you have managed to turn that into a decent living and now live a wealthy life. Whatever your circumstances, we have all faced challenges and hardships, but we have come out the other side. And the lessons that you have learned along the way may be part of who you are today, and the experiences may be what you enjoyed the most about your journey.

Even though you may have enjoyed those experiences, they were likely tough. Would you want your kids to go through the same thing to get to where they want to be? Most parents would probably say no; they don't want their kids to have to suffer as they did. But at the same time, you want them to have experiences, learn, and grow.

But is there a middle ground? The middle ground is investing in your kids, provided they invest in themselves. Let's take a bicycle as an example. A younger kid may want a bicycle. Tell them you will pay for two-thirds of the bike if they invest in themselves and pay for the other third. They can do this by earning money doing chores around the house. As your kids get older, you can follow the same principles when they want to make more significant purchases, such as a car. By asking them to invest in themselves, they are still experiencing some of the struggles that you went through, but it won't be as rough a ride as it was for you. They will also learn to appreciate money a lot more than if you simply give them the bike or the car for nothing. There is some sort of gratification for making it on your own and your kids will feel like they accomplished this by earning their part of the purchase.

You can also talk about investing in your kids' education. For instance, if a child is genuinely talented, extra music or drama lessons are an investment in their future - not an indulgence; but to afford them, your youngster might have to give up some other things. So talk about the concept of education and getting qualifications, or learning skills, as an investment in the future.

RULE NUMBER 17: IT'S NOT OVER TILL IT'S OVER

The thing with money talk is that you can't just do it the once. You have to keep repeating the lessons over and over, until well, forever. But, even after they have flown the nest, you can still help your kids make good money decisions. Think about how great it would feel if, when your kids have their own families, they tell their children, "Go talk to your grandparents about how to manage your money; they're really good at it!" And if you have done a good job, hopefully, your words will guide them even after you have left this earth.

Conversations about the meaning and significance of money and wealth are the kind of ones that we need to continue having for the rest of our lives.

The remaining chapters in this book talk about what you can teach children at each age. Bear in mind that kids mature at different ages - Mozart and cellist Yo-Yo Ma were playing in public at the age of five, and drumming prodigy Nandi Bushell performed onstage with Foo Fighters in 2021, aged just eleven, while some kids never learn to carry a tune. That's the same with finance - some children will already be asking questions about how the stock market works when they're nine or ten; others will not even have their act together when it comes to savings at that age. So, if your child has already done all the activities for their age and has a good understanding of the concepts we've presented, they can progress on to the next chapter, even if it's a year or two early. Equally, some children may take a while to learn particular concepts and habits, and that's okay.

WHEN YOUR KIDS ARE THREE OR FOUR

YOUNG KIDS DON'T REALLY UNDERSTAND MONEY. Dorothy singer, ed.d., a senior research scientist at yale university, tells parents, "A two- or three-year-old faced with a choice between a penny, dime and nickel will almost always choose the nickel because of its size." They have a lot to learn!

Younger kids are still getting their act together. They live in the moment a lot and have difficulty waiting for things; they don't understand the idea of delayed gratification. But they are beginning to understand that you exchange money for things. And because this tends to be an age when kids are super curious about everything, you can use this to your advantage when teaching them about money.

If you have a three-year-old, you've probably already noticed them starting to ask lots of questions!

Use this as an opportunity. At this age, it's best to take more of a playful approach; investigate and play with everything and encourage them to start learning about money.

While very young children won't fully understand the value of money, they can begin to handle money and learn the names of the different coins and notes.

They should be able to recognize different coins by their numbers, color, or shape.

They should also be able to understand that things cost different amounts, such as a new toy or a soda, and that some things cost more than others. By age 3, they should also start to learn that money needs to be kept safe so that it doesn't get lost.

Most of the ways you will teach your kids about money at this age will be through play. You might want to use something other than real money for a pretend store - tokens, big plastic coins, LEGO bricks, or vouchers. As kids get older, you can use real money.

Take care if you have babies or toddlers in the family. For example, when you're using coins for activities with your three or four-year-old, make sure they're tidied away afterward; they're too easy for a little one to swallow or choke on.

FUN ACTIVITIES AT HOME

FUN ACTIVITY - SHOPPING LIST

Let them help you make the shopping list and then tell them how much each item costs when you go to the store. This is a good time to talk about how sometimes we only have money for what we need, such as basic food, but not for treats like cake or candies. So they start to learn that as adults, we sometimes have to make choices.

FUN ACTIVITY – COIN-COUNTING

Get some 1 cent coins. Count out different amounts with them and when they count correctly, reward them with an extra cent in their piggy bank. As they get older and better at this, you might use bigger coins, so their piggy bank is worth a bit more.

FUN ACTIVITY - COIN STACKING

Get some coins of different values. Build piles of them next to each other to show your kids the different values. Then, knock them down and ask them to recreate them. This can help with muscle control and concentration as well as understanding money - it's not easy to build a pile of twenty pennies without knocking them over!

FUN ACTIVITY – PRETEND STORE

Set up a pretend store at home. Add labels to household items and add them to the store. Set a budget and take it in turns to be the buyer. Help them work out what they can buy with the money they have.

You don't have to use real money for this activity. Instead, you could use tokens, LEGO bricks, or beans. The whole idea is to get your kids used to the concept of exchanging a 'currency' of whatever sort for real things and the idea that those things have different values.

FUN ACTIVITY – COIN IDENTIFICATION

Play the coin identification game. First, work with your child to trace the shape of the coins onto a piece of paper. Then jumble the coins up and ask them to put each coin back inside the correct circle. Teach them the names of the coins as you go along.

FUN ACTIVITY - WHAT'S ON THE BANKNOTE?

Talk about what's shown on both sides of banknotes. Talk about how to tell one note from another. You might draw your own notes - you could copy a dollar bill or a five-pound note, or you could make up your own home currency for the pretend store.

FUN ACTIVITY - MARSHMALLOW CHALLENGE

This can help children learn how to wait for things. For example, give them a marshmallow (or a cookie) and say, "I've got to do something in the kitchen and I'm going to leave you here for five minutes. Then, if you don't eat that marshmallow and you can show it to me when I come back, I'll give you another one as well."

Start with just a few minutes. It's really hard at first, so don't be too hard on your kid, and once they manage to wait the time out, plenty of praise and affirmation is in order.

FUN ACTIVITIES OUT AND ABOUT

FUN ACTIVITY - HELP WITH SHOPPING

Ask your kids to load the shopping items onto the belt once you get to the checkout. Then, give the money to them so that they can pay the shop assistant. They'll feel responsible and grown-up and should hopefully be paying attention to how much everyday things cost.

Show them how you check the change and the receipt. They won't be able to work this out themselves yet, but it's important that you show them. If you pay by card, ask them if you have remembered to take your card, because that's important.

WHEN YOUR KIDS ARE FIVE OR SIX

BY NOW, YOUR CHILD HAS STARTED SCHOOL AND WILL be learning lots of new things, including starting to have a deeper understanding of numbers through the games they do at school. They should also be able to pay attention for longer, which makes a great opportunity for playing games to demonstrate to them about money management.

They'll be able to understand that:

- $ The different coins have different values
- $ Many pennies create pounds/dollars
- $ Saving money can help them buy things they want
- $ They need to keep money safe from being lost or from others taking it
- $ Needs and wants are different
- $ If people lose money, it can upset them

$ Some money can't be seen (virtual money, bank balance)

$ They can earn money, for instance, by doing chores

AT HOME

Learning can be more structured now they're a little older and you can take advantage of what they've learned so far. They will learn the most from watching and listening, so take advantage of these techniques. Some useful ones include:

$ Role-playing. You might replay the conversation you had with the teller in your bank branch or with the cashier in a supermarket.

$ When they overhear you talking about money, ask them if they have any questions about money. Explain in terms they can understand; for instance, if you lease your car, you can tell them that you have to pay every month for it - they won't be able to understand all the details though.

$ When money or financial transactions are shown on the TV or in films, ask them questions about what's going on and why.

$ Explain that not everything costs money. Ask them which free activities they enjoy. Visit a local free library or the park and ask if it's as much fun as buying a book or going to a paid-for attraction and why.

At this age, children will be starting to understand the idea of saving money for the things you want, so you should encourage them to do so. This will help them with patience and with the ability to make decisions about medium-term targets. First, however, make the target close enough in time that they can visualize it and easily see the steps they are making towards it.

OUT AND ABOUT

You may need to rethink some of your regular habits to help your kids. For example, using the self-checkout at the supermarket may work for you, but it's not as useful as using the cashier as a teaching method for your kids. You may usually use the ATM, but you probably want to take your children to a bank branch so they can see a face-to-face transaction, which is easier for them to understand.

You can maybe pay them a small allowance and they can save towards a new toy. Buy games that you can play with them that teach about numbers or using money. Play games when you go out shopping so that they're aware of what you're using money for.

Children need to start developing willpower and the ability to wait at this age, which can be a tough challenge. Many kids will pester their parents for anything they want at this age. Teaching them about the difference between wants and needs can help them understand why they can't always have everything they want.

When you go out shopping, tell them what you're going to buy beforehand. They can help you make the list; ask if you forgot anything. Or ask if you had forgotten to put something basic on there, like toilet paper or bread, would they have noticed when it ran out?

If they ask for things, listen to them and empathize with them, but explain that they may need to wait until their birthday or till the holidays. Explain why they can't have everything now, by pointing out that we have needs and sometimes we only have money for these. Talk about some choices you've had to make - not buying a new outfit or a new car. This will also help them understand that we have to make choices with money as adults.

I should stress that it's very important that you always stick to your word. Your children need to know that their patience has been rewarded if they wait for something or save for it. So don't use things they want as a kind of blackmail ("If you're not good, you won't get that bicycle"). And if you've promised to match their savings, make sure that you will be financially able to do so. Otherwise, what they'll learn is that waiting for things doesn't work and that they can't trust anyone - not the lessons you want them to learn.

DISCUSSION – WANTS AND NEEDS

You need to start having this discussion with kids about this age. Explain to them which things you need - real basics. You could start on the level of 'somewhere to sleep, enough food to eat.' Then talk about the basics on the shopping list, like toilet paper, bread/rice/potatoes, vegetables. And then talk about wants, like sweets, toys, or particular breakfast cereal brands.

You don't need to be too heavy-handed, but if there's a news report of a hurricane affecting a state, or flooding, you can ask about what those people need - and whether their needs are being met. Then, if you have enough money, you might decide to donate to a fund to help out, showing your children how having money lets you help other people.

But you also need to make sure you're not implying there's anything wrong with wants. It's just a question of priorities. You have to make sure that everything you need is covered before looking at the other options.

FUN ACTIVITIES AT HOME

FUN ACTIVITY – FAMILY SAVING

Ask them if there is something they would like to save for that the whole family can benefit from. For instance, a weekend at the beach or a tree for the garden. Ask them to draw a picture of the thing they want. Then ask how they can save to pay for it.

Let them manage the savings in their piggy bank so that they can see it grow - or watch the total grow online. It can be particularly powerful to draw a chart of the money or a load of dollar bills or pound coins around the picture of the objective. Then, when you have saved enough, go out and buy the treat with them and praise them!

FUN ACTIVITY - SAVING AROUND THE HOUSE

Together, think of ideas to save money. For instance, can you buy a cheaper breakfast cereal? Could you grow your own salad in the garden? Talk about the difference between branded goods and supermarket white-label goods, such as washing up liquid or toothpaste. You can discuss whether the more expensive item is sometimes worth it and how it's worth trying cheaper products to see the difference.

Don't make this just an exercise in penny-pinching. That's not a great message to give your children - even if you really do need to make economies. Instead, make it a chance to talk about priorities. For instance, "If we gave up eating fruit, we'd save that money on the shopping. But would it be good for us? How else could we save that money?"

Use a picture of the house to draw all the places you can save money - light bulbs, the fridge, wherever.

This exercise can start simple and then you can make it more complex as your children get older and understand a bit more.

FUN ACTIVITY – A PENNY HUNT

Treasure hunts of any kind are fun for kids. At its simplest, just hide pennies around the house and go and find them together, or let your child look for them in the room and give 'hot' and 'cold' hints depending on how close they are.

You can make it a bit more difficult by giving hints or clues, like "change the channel and find the penny" (hidden under the TV remote) or "will it become a chicken?" (under the eggs in the fridge). Make some easy and some more challenging so that some of the pennies are easy to find, but your kids will have to work harder for the others. Of course, you can always help them with the clues - if they ask nicely!

FUN ACTIVITY – PLAY 'SHOP'

Setting up a play 'store' is fun, particularly if kids have made the things they will sell. For instance, one little boy set up a tea shop and made cupcakes with his mom to sell to other family members. Or it can all be "let's pretend" or set up using real goods from the kitchen cabinet.

Let kids play the different roles. They can be the store owner, but they can also be the customer. Why don't you be the child and let them be the parent and explain to you how to go shopping properly?

As they get older, you can have fun by making mistakes with your money and let them point out that you've got it wrong. Kids absolutely love it when they can get one up on mom or dad!

FUN ACTIVITY – IMAGINARY RESTAURANT

Kids love playing this game. It encourages many skills, not just financial – setting the table, serving food, and table manners. Of course, you may have to remind them after the meal that it needs to be paid for, but once they understand the concept of having to pay, they'll be excited about paying with pretend money.

Again, they can play different roles - a diner, a waiter, the restaurant owner, a chef (maybe the chef has to be paid out of the waiter's money! You can develop these games a little bit further whenever you think your child is ready for a new concept).

FUN ACTIVITIES OUT AND ABOUT

FUN ACTIVITY – FINDING THE BARGAINS

Kids love a challenge. Can they help you save money on your grocery shop? So, for instance, can they find the cheapest tin of beans? The cheapest washing-up liquid? Can they find a two-for-one offer? Is there a bargain/short-dated goods area? Right now, your kids' math probably isn't good enough to calculate which are the best offers, but give them some help hunting down bargains and if they've made a difference, share it with them - either by buying them a small treat or by giving them some money to put in their savings.

FUN ACTIVITY – WHAT CAN YOU GET FOR A DOLLAR?

This is good fun for kids. Give them just one dollar for their own shopping. They can buy anything with that dollar, but they can't pay any more than a dollar. So what can they purchase with it?

Again, you may need to help with the math, but you're teaching the basic principles. First of all, your kids are getting a feeling for how much things cost - that you can buy the two-pack of Reese's Peanut Butter Cups for less than a dollar, but not a big box of them, for instance. And secondly, they're getting used to having to make choices. You might want to introduce saving as another option for the dollar at a certain stage, so your child could decide to save the dollar for next time and then get something for two dollars.

FUN ACTIVITY – BUYING SCHOOL LUNCH

If kids take their own lunch to school, you can set a budget in your grocery shop for the materials for their lunches for the week. You can then get them to help you choose the items, but they have to fit in the budget. You're teaching a lot with this one. You're teaching about choice. You're teaching about value. And you can also use it to teach about healthy eating.

Suppose your child decides to spend the whole budget on candy and cookies, even after you've talked about healthy eating? Well, maybe let them do it - once. And when they come home, serve up candies and cookies instead of dinner. And instead of breakfast. They'll probably make a different decision next time!

FUN ACTIVITY - WHAT'S THE PRICE?

When you're out shopping, you can ask your kids to shout out the price of each product you're putting in the trolley. This can be a fun game for younger kids.

FUN ACTIVITY – PLAIN OR PRETTY?

Start explaining branding by showing your kids the cheaper alternative to the bright, sparkly packages or the expensive branded pack. What's inside? Is it different or the same? Often, the cheap pack is pretty much the same. But sometimes it isn't. For instance, in some cases, the more expensive packet has more in it, or the more expensive fruit juice is 100% juice and the cheap one isn't.

By looking at different goods each time you go to the store, your kids will appreciate that they need to make value judgments for themselves and look actively for the best deal.

FUN ACTIVITY – COUPON CUTTING

Before heading to the grocery store, ask your children to help you cut out coupons (don't forget to use child-friendly scissors). Or you might look for voucher codes on the internet. Then, when you're at the store, let them look after the coupons and ask them to look out for the products in the shop. This will make them feel like they're helping, and they'll feel all grown up and responsible. Use it as an opportunity to talk about ways to save money.

WHEN YOUR KIDS ARE SEVEN OR EIGHT

WHAT YOUR KIDS KNOW
AT THIS AGE

BY THIS AGE, YOUR KIDS SHOULD HAVE DEVELOPED AN understanding of the difference between needs and wants. They should also be aware of ways of paying for things that don't involve the exchange of cash, such as paying for something online, using your card, using an app, or doing bank transfers. they should also have a good grasp of the need to keep track of what we spend on things and the importance of saving. Some children at this age will have an awareness of lending and borrowing as well; if not, it's important that they now start to learn about the topic.

You can build on all the knowledge they already have to help them make good decisions about money, spending and saving, and encourage them to form lasting good habits. So much of what you'll be doing now goes into greater depth and more detail and reinforces the good habits they've already begun to acquire.

Children are still developing willpower at this age and learning that they have to wait for certain things. However, they are learning that they can delay having something now for something better later on once they have saved.

By this age, they know your weak spots and can really take advantage of you if you crumble when faced with temptation. So, set them a good example and avoid making impulse purchases yourself, or you will have them decide to make their own impulse purchases - but at your expense!

ALLOWANCES AND CHORES

If you're paying your child an allowance or pocket money, you may want to increase it at this age. For example, you may be paying them according to their age, so $7 per month or £7 may be appropriate and will give them more responsibility for their actions with money. Or you might just look at what they are buying for themselves and set a reasonable budget. If your children are buying their own lunches, for instance, you'll want to give them more than if you provide a packed lunch.

It's a good idea to ask them to do small chores around the house in exchange for their allowance so that they can learn that things don't come for free, and they can spend their own money on things they want, rather than your money! However, you need to avoid giving the impression that you don't help other family members unless it's paid for in a household.

For instance, if your children regularly help in the kitchen, don't start paying them for that. Instead, find them a spring-cleaning chore, something to do in the garden, or ask for help with the washing. Doing the washing up or stacking the dishwasher, on the other hand, is something you do because you care for other members of the family. You may want to talk that over with your kids.

Saving, spending, and giving boxes are ideal for separating out the different uses for money and teaching them that we don't just spend all our money.

You may even want to take a trip to the bank with them to open a small savings account to encourage them to make regular deposits. Many banks have child-friendly accounts with no fee or minimum balance. Opening an account early on has considerable advantages in getting your kids to regard banking as a normal part of their lives, and it will help them learn about basic account management. It's also good to get grandparents and other family members to put a little money in the kids' accounts on birthdays and Christmas.

MANAGING PEER PRESSURE

By this age, if not before, kids start to want what every other kid in their class has. Crazes go around schools and all of a sudden, every kid needs to have the latest must-have toy, game, or trainers.

Peer pressure is starting to play an important part in their lives. But how can you manage this? On the one hand, you don't want them missing out and becoming the lonely kid who sticks out like a sore thumb, but you also don't want them to think they can have everything they want just because everyone else has it. And in fact, you don't want them to assume that other people should set their goals or that following the crowd is always the correct answer.

So it's good to start talking about self-discipline and also about creating their own identity. When they ask for something because everyone else at school has it, maybe ask them a few questions – what does it mean to them to have the same as their friends? What do they have that their friends don't have, and why do they want what their friends have? This will help you see their motives for wanting the latest item.

Talk about the value of the item - what you would have to pay for it, how long it will last, the way people sometimes use particular items as a 'badge' for their membership in a group and the idea of 'brand value.' You might, for instance, look at the difference between the low, middle, and high-priced versions of the same food in the supermarket or the difference in quality between Adidas and unbranded trainers. Sometimes, the expensive thing will be better made or contain better ingredients - and sometimes it won't. You could also explore what apps and games they can get as free or 'freemium' compared to paid-for.

Having these chats about peer pressure can also be a good time to start to explain the differences in wealth between your family and others - for instance, that because you work in a social enterprise, you don't make as much money as parents who own their own businesses or work as managers in big companies. You might also talk about inherited wealth at this point.

Concentrate on asking questions rather than just saying "yes" or "no." Obviously, you have your household budget to meet, but the point of the discussion isn't to make a decision - it's to help your child understand how to make decisions themselves.

They will make plenty of mistakes along the way. Sometimes, they'll cave in to peer pressure and maybe regret it later - but this is all part of the learning experience and growing up.

Of course, you can also talk about the needs/wants decisions that you've made yourself. For instance, you might have decided to do without a car or have an older and smaller car than most of your friends to use the money on something else. Or you might have used a bonus from your employer to pay for a 'luxury' for yourself.

TALKING ABOUT MONEY AT HOME

At this age, you may want to pass the decision to them over how they look after their money; do they want to keep it at home in jars, or do they want to open a bank account? Do they need anything to carry it in when they take it out with them? Some children may want a small bag or wallet. Some kids may want to have a jar to save up to a particular value and then take it to the bank. There's no single 'right answer.'

Help them think about what they want to save for and how long it will take. At this age, they will be able to understand that if they put it in the bank, it may earn a little bit of interest and so grow in value, so let them make that decision.

It's also a good idea to go online and show them how a bank account works. Many of us are very wary of answering children's questions about our household finances – no-one wants children in the playground screaming "My dad earns $150,000 a year!" or "We've got a bigger mortgage than yours" at each other. But it's important to treat finance as something that's normal and introduce the idea that it's something you can, and should, talk about in a household. So you might choose to just look at your savings account, for instance.

Many of our purchases nowadays are made online and as adults, we know how easy it is to get carried away on online spending sprees. It is important that we teach our kids that we must think carefully before buying online as we can get carried away and spend money we don't always have. Go online with them and make a purchase, but explain that you must always supervise them to make online purchases until they're older.

TALKING ABOUT MONEY OUT AND ABOUT

After a few years at school, children should be starting to get a better grasp of numbers and you can play fun games while out shopping. Ask them to help you compare prices between the own brands and the major brands. Talk to them about how you can save money in the shops by looking for reasonable offers - buy one get one free, two for the price of one, discounted goods, or bulk buys.

It would help if you also started discussing the adverts that you see for different products. First, explain to your children that companies advertise to make products more appealing to people and to encourage them to buy them. Next, ask your kids if they have ever bought something they wanted that wasn't as good as they expected. Why not? How could they have found that out? Finally, look at some online reviews, for instance, on Amazon, to see how you might research a product before making a decision.

This is also the right time to start talking about the differences between buying and borrowing and the advantages and disadvantages of both. For instance, instead of buying a book, can it be borrowed from the local library? What are the advantages? It's free, instead of paying for it; if you read a lot, it can save big money; it can let you try out things that you're not sure you'd like. And the disadvantages? You can't make notes in the book; you have to look after it carefully; you have to remember when to take it back; you might not be able to borrow the book you want if someone else has taken it out; you can't keep it like you can your favorite books, so you can't re-read it any time you want.

If you have a DIY project and you rent a tool to do the job, that can be a great time to explain about 'borrowing' in the grown-up world, too.

FUN ACTIVITIES AT HOME

FUN ACTIVITY – NEEDS AND WANTS

Draw a picture of people's needs and wants. Let them be creative and have fun with different colored pens and crayons or make a collage with pictures out of a magazine. Consider different people - a baby, a child the same age as yours, someone your age, someone your grandparents' age. Are their needs the same? Do they have very different wants?

FUN ACTIVITY - PRETEND YOU'RE GOING TO A DESERT ISLAND

You can each take seven items with you. Choose your items and write them down. It's even more fun for kids if you're not allowed to look at what they're writing - it has to be secret! Or you can set a timer for five minutes to introduce a bit of time pressure. Then, compare your lists.

Did you miss out something obvious? (remember, kids love it so much when their parents make a mistake, so forget something that's crucial, or take something that needs to be plugged in to the electricity to make it work). What did you want to put on the list but didn't? Did you take something that isn't going to be of any use, or that's just silly?

Explain how we have to make choices in life with what we buy even when we aren't going to a desert island.

FUN ACTIVITY - A DESERT ISLAND AT HOME

This exercise also addresses the difficulties of choosing when your 'budget' is limited. You can play a couple of versions. Imagine you're being taken to the desert island for a week and you have to pack 7 things each and you have to be able to put all of them in one supermarket bag. What do you take?

Or you could put price tags on things around the house and give your kids a budget. Then, they can choose whatever fits within that budget (it's always fun if you set it so that they can't take, for instance, both a blanket and a pillow).

And again, you can play this as a timed challenge to grab what you can - the pirate ship is coming in five minutes, you need to get ready!

FUN ACTIVITY - MARSHMALLOW CHALLENGE STEP-UP

Some kids may not have had the willpower to play this test up till now. Others will be looking to take a step up and have to resist for a longer time.

A really good version is the box of Maltesers or other small candies. First, take all the candies out of the box except one. Then, add a candy for every five minutes they avoid eating the first one. It's a great exercise because seeing the box fill up gradually is a powerful way to visualize the way savings work - but it's also more and more tempting to eat one of the candies! If they get to ten, you can add a bonus as 'interest' on the candy savings account.

You can have a more in-depth conversation about savings by now than you did when they were younger and talk about the rewards for saving. Of course, this is too young for most children to talk about compounding, but they can get the basic idea that the longer, and the more, you save, the more your savings will grow.

FUN ACTIVITY - THE SNACK SHOP

If you're being eaten out of house and home with all the snacks your kids are eating, turn it into a game. Put a price list of all the snack items together and give them a daily budget. The prices don't have to be in real money - you can make your own currency and 'charge' them in that. This gives you a bit of extra power - if you want to encourage your children to eat healthily, you can set the healthier items at lower prices, which might not be the case in the supermarket.

This activity will help them to understand that we have to make choices with money and that once you've spent it, it's gone - you don't get a second chance!

FUN ACTIVITY - COIN COLLECTING

Kids this age often begin to get interested in collecting things, so you could suggest coin collecting as a fascinating hobby. Visit the US Mint website – **www.usmint.gov/kids** so that they can learn the history and evolution of the US dollar. Talk about different countries' money if you go on vacation abroad.

FUN ACTIVITY - SAVING UP FOR SOMETHING

This builds on the earlier exercise of saving up for something the family will enjoy, but in greater depth. Talk to them about something they really want, but they don't have enough money for from their spending jar. Help them to work out the math - how long will it take them to have enough money to buy it? Set up a saving chart to track how much they have each week and see themselves moving closer to their goal.

Put milestones at 25%, 50%, 75% so they can see how close they are getting - and also treat them to an ice cream or some candy when they reach the milestones. Remember to praise them when they reach their goal; as for many kids, it's a real struggle for the first time they do this. And let them pay for their purchase themselves - they will be really proud of themselves!

FUN ACTIVITY - REVIEW YOUR CHOICES!

Go into your child's room and ask them to get out all the things they've bought over the past few years that they thought were 'must-haves.' Ask them which ones they still love, whether they still use them.

If the answer's yes, then that was a good decision. If the answer's no, then maybe it wasn't. Talk about why they don't use or want it anymore. It might simply be because they've grown up and it's not interesting (or in the case of clothes, doesn't fit them) anymore. It might be because the 'craze' has passed by. They might not have thought through the purchase decision for one toy or game and then have been disappointed as soon as they got it out of its box.

Could they have saved up for something better? Do they wish they'd bought something else instead?

It's very easy to be judgmental and you should resist the temptation. We all make mistakes, particularly when we are just getting started on something. I'm sure you can think of people who joined a gym or took up a new hobby, but after a while found it didn't suit them. The important thing is that they get used to thinking about these issues. Next time they make a decision, they'll have a structure for thinking through their choices.

FUN ACTIVITIES OUT AND ABOUT

FUN ACTIVITY - BUDGET YOUR WEEKEND

You probably don't want to do this every weekend, but it's a great exercise for weekends out. Sit down with your child and list the things you'll be doing over the weekend: going to the park, going to an event, or a museum, eating out. Then think about the smaller items, like snacks and drinks, transport costs, and so on. Make a budget and give your child just enough cash to cover the costs. They're then responsible for paying all the bills.

If they ask for something that wasn't budgeted for, you'll need to explain that this could mean you will have to cut out something else. You might work out a new choice - for instance, buy the theatre program, but don't have a starter or dessert with your meal - but it still has to be within budget. Or you might 'lend' money, but in that case, it has to be repaid out of their money jar or savings when you get back.

FUN ACTIVITY - SAVE, SAVE, SAVE!

Depending on your child's mathematical abilities and confidence, this can be good fun every time you go shopping. Give them a task, such as "buy the best value toilet tissue" or "find the cheapest way for us to buy tomato ketchup," or "look at the shopping list and see if any of the things we need are discounted." Point out any tags that show you how much a product costs per pint or per pound; the packet that costs least may not be the best value. It can be a good idea to take a calculator or use the calculator on your mobile phone to get them used to working out unit prices.

You might also discuss where you made the most significant savings. On some other items, the difference between the cheapest and most expensive brand might not be very great at all, so maybe it's not worth trying to save a lot next time. The reward, of course, is a cut of the savings!

FUN ACTIVITY - THE UTILITY BILL

You may not think the utility bill can be fun, but kids can be surprisingly motivated if you go through the bills and explain that you'll let them have a share of any savings they can suggest.

Show how the particular tariff that you're on works; for instance, you may have a standard monthly charge plus a per-unit charge or a per-unit charge over a certain amount of usage. First, check if the bill is correct. Then find a comparison website like powerswitch.com and see if you can get a better deal.

You could also use shopzilla.com to look at comparisons for appliances, electricals and so on, as well as clothes.

WHEN YOUR KIDS ARE NINE TO TWELVE

BY THE TIME CHILDREN GET TO THIS AGE, THEY HAVE started to want more independence and want to hang out with their friends without their embarrassing parents lurking in the background. but if they want to hang out with their friends, they will normally need money so that they can go off and do fun things such as bowling or going to the movies. If you've already gone through all the steps in this book with them at each age, they should be ready for this, and you should have a good feeling for how much money you can entrust them with.

As they become more independent, it is important that you keep talking about money with them. Now they're going to understand a lot more about it. For instance, you can talk about interest rates. You might spot a bank ad with a considerable interest rate marked on it; then, when you get home, you can build a spreadsheet with them to show how interest rates work and how over several years, the amount of money in the account will increase as the first year's interest will get interest paid on it too in year two. That's the effect of compounding.

If math is not your kid's strong suit, just use 10% as the interest rate and $100 or $1000 as the starting amount to make it easy for them.

And, of course, you need to continue your work to help your kids acquire good money habits, which they'll then take into adult life with them.

WHAT YOUR KIDS KNOW AT THIS AGE

By this age, kids have a longer attention span and will understand a lot more about money. They will be able to do simple calculations, know about different currencies used in other countries, learn how to make simple budgets, how to save and keep track of what they're spending.

They should be able to check any bank statements, bills, or receipts laying around the house and understand what some of the numbers mean. They will have a good awareness of advertising and what its purpose is. You've also shown them how to compare the prices of different products and to make better choices.

They should by now have a good understanding of how to make a purchase online. Although, now they're becoming more independent, you need to teach them more about the risk of scams and how to avoid them. You should also talk about making sure they are not trapped into a subscription service without realizing it and about verifying the total price before they buy.

Many kids will have a bank account of some sort at this age and will understand bank interest and the importance of saving. However, they must realize that saving isn't just 'a good thing' in itself, but because it allows them to have things they wouldn't be able to afford straight away. You can work with them more on planning their savings goals at this age, and since they now have a better idea of what their future lives might contain, you can start talking about slightly longer-term targets. Being able to buy a much-wanted item also brings children a sense of achievement, which you can increase even more by remembering to tell them how well they have done and celebrating that achievement with them.

Keep helping your kids to see the importance of making choices – to buy or not to buy, to save or spend, to buy the more expensive or less expensive item, to give their time to someone rather than buying them an expensive gift, not to buy something just because all their friends have it. By now, if you have a purchase coming up - new appliances, a new car, some crafting supplies, or books - kids are old enough that you can talk to them about that decision in some detail.

ALLOWANCES

At this age, it is a good opportunity to really instill into them good money management practices and make them responsible for a greater percentage of spending. For instance, they may be mature enough to make their own decisions on some items of clothing, on their mobile apps and spending, and so on. But, of course, that means you'll likely be paying them a higher allowance.

Talk through what you expect in return for the allowance. That might be keeping their room tidy, helping with the chores, or seeing their grandparents every second weekend. Have this conversation upfront - don't use it as blackmail, just remind them gently if they are beginning to let their standards slide. For example, you might compare their allowance with your salary at this age - your employer has expectations that you have to meet. Although, of course, you need to reassure them that yes, you are still a parent, not an employer, and yes, you do still love them unconditionally.

If you haven't already set up a bank account for them, you probably want to get started now. For example, you might set up a prepaid card account with GoHenry (in both USA and UK) or Famzoo and encourage them to save as well as spend. This is also a good age to teach them about giving money away to good causes as part of their budget. At this age, kids may be particularly interested in wildlife charities, for instance, or you can make things 'personal' by sponsoring a particular village project.

No matter how big or small the allowance (and this may depend on your affordability, of course), the lessons an allowance teaches your kids are invaluable. It teaches them how to manage money, save, and make choices on what to spend their money on.

Your kids may even decide they want to contribute to family expenses if it gives them expanded choices, for instance, paying some of the TV subs to get a Disney+ subscription or paying towards video game passes.

Divvying money up into different pots can be done in apps like RoosterMoney, which also lets you set chore lists and give to charity. Even better, if you're in the UK, you can link a prepaid debit card to this app so that your child can use it to spend when out and about.

They can't run up bills over a certain limit because it's prepaid, and you get alerts whenever they spend so that you are aware of what they're spending money on (for younger kids, there is the option to award stars which can progress into money later).

You might decide to start a GoHenry or RoosterMoney account with a week's or a month's allowance. Childrens' maturity and their ability to deal with being paid a month's money at once can differ. If you pay them a month, and they run out of money, they've learned a lesson. But you should ask them why they didn't manage their money better. Sometimes the answer may be that they had to help out a friend by lending them some money or that they had forgotten to budget for a certain item. That's not so bad. If the answer is "I just couldn't help myself," on the other hand, you might want to ask if they'd be happier being paid weekly for the time being.

If you give them a weekly allowance, you could save the treats for special occasions such as birthday and Christmas. You could also give them chances to earn more money by doing jobs around the house - at this age, they'll be able to do a lot more, such as washing the car, mowing the lawn, or helping with DIY projects. Letting them help with a yard sale can also earn money by selling toys and clothes they're too old for.

Giving them these extra opportunities to earn will help them see that they can work harder to save more money and save more quickly so that they can buy the things they want (make sure you set an upper limit on what they can earn so that they can see that you are managing your own finances. However, it might be fun to let them mow the lawn every day for a week the first time, even though it doesn't need it, because they're always going to remember how they outsmarted you).

Make sure you're clear on what they need to earn and what items you will pay for so that you set clear boundaries. That's going to be really good for them later on when, maybe, they need to negotiate with a partner or spouse about what they pay for in common and what each of them has discretion to spend. It's also useful when they get to work and need to divide work expenses from personal expenses.

For example, if they want to do activities with their friends, up till now, you may have paid for sports subscriptions and weekend events out of your own pocket. Maybe now, it's time to give them more independence. That means a bigger allowance, but it also means they can't ask you to pay for things unless they are really exceptional.

BUILDING RESPONSIBILITY AROUND MONEY

Most kids will start to want a mobile phone at this age and their friends will also likely start to get them (in fact, the age that kids get a mobile keeps going down all the time, so even younger kids may have one). Use buying a phone as an opportunity to talk about the financial responsibility of having a phone. Do they know how much phones cost or how much it costs to use the phone? How does pay as you go work? How does it work if you're on a contract and what are the costs involved? What happens if they use up all their credit or lose the phone?

And obviously, you're going to want to talk through the decision of which phone or package to buy. Though you might change the way you're doing this for older kids - ask them to come up with a report that looks at three or four different packages and gives you a recommendation for what they want. You can say that's very similar to the way a start-up business produces a business plan to get funding - it's quite a grown-up way to do things.

Set up some rules around money and safety. For example, do you want to set an allowance each month and once credit runs out, they have to wait until the start of the following month? What happens if they lose the phone? Will you buy a new one or will they have to wait until their birthday to replace it? You might talk about phone insurance or whether you could lend them the money to buy a new phone and set monthly or weekly repayments.

Encourage them to create a budget or plan to help them look after their money. They could write down what they're saving for and keep track of it or keep it on a spreadsheet. Show them how to record how much money they have and record it decreasing as they spend it or increasing as they save. Review this with them regularly, maybe monthly. Ask them about the plan, have they made any notes, is it going up or down? Decide what happens if they go over their budget.

TEACH THEM
ABOUT BORROWING

This is a good age to start teaching them about borrowing money and letting them know that borrowing means they will have to pay it back at some point, maybe with interest. It's time to teach them how to schedule repayments. Remember, you already helped them save over a much longer period - starting from just a week or so and working up to several months or even a year for a much bigger purchase. So now, you're doing the same for loans, starting with borrowing an amount that needs to be repaid next week but thinking about loans that might last longer.

They should be old enough to understand that borrowing is like the reverse of saving - instead of getting paid interest, they'll pay interest to the bank.

Find opportunities to ask them questions about their understanding of borrowing. When you see bank ads, when neighbors move house (or you do), or if you lease a new car, these are all great occasions to talk about the benefits of borrowing - and the downsides. Why would they want to borrow? What would they do if they couldn't pay it back? Are there any ways to avoid having to borrow money? This should get them thinking creatively about money and seeing the importance of saving.

START TALKING ABOUT HOW BUSINESS WORKS

It's time kids got an idea of how a business works. If you own your own business or freelance, you can show them exactly how it works for you. This isn't just about taking them to the office or letting them see a building site; it's about showing them how money is made. So, for instance, if you're a building contractor, show them the difference between working as a subcontractor or running your own project. If you run a restaurant, start showing them the bills, the bookings, and how much your ingredients cost.

If certain trades are shown on TV, ask how people make money in that business. Do they get paid for the hours they work? Do they make a margin on selling products that they've bought for resale? Do they make their products from raw materials, then sell them for a profit?

You might also watch series like Flea Market Flip, Pawn Stars, Auction Hunters, or The Apprentice. They can be a bit contrived and theatrical, but they're a great way to start a discussion.

FUN ACTIVITIES AT HOME

FUN ACTIVITY - 'BUSINESS PLAN' YOUR NEXT BIG PURCHASE

Let them think of something they want, whether that be the latest gadget all their friends have or a new pair of trainers. How much does the item cost? Ask them how they can get that amount of money. Tell them to write down their income and how much they could realistically save towards this item. Get them to come up with creative ideas of how they could earn more money to put towards it. Once they've hit their goal, get them to set a bigger challenge and think of even more ways to save.

FUN ACTIVITY - MONEY GAMES

Why not get out a board game that you can all play together? Monopoly was invented in 1935, but it's still the obvious choice if you want your kids to learn about money using board games. You can turn it into a lesson about rent and mortgages and going bankrupt - and also about risk (do you or don't you buy Mayfair if that means you have almost no money left?). The junior version is short and sweet. Game of Life and Catan are also great for money lessons, and for more advanced subjects, there's The Stock Exchange Game and Thrive Time.

FUN ACTIVITY - COMPOUNDING

Teach your kids about the power of compounding. For example, ask them if they would rather be given £500 a day for thirty days or start with a penny and double it every day for sixty days. Then, get them to work out what would give them more money. Work it out at ten-day intervals and ask if they want to change their answer.

You might also look at the famous chess board problem. A king offered the architect who had built his palace a reward. The architect said, "I want a chessboard, with one dollar on the first square, two dollars on the second square, four dollars on the next," and so on - doubling every time. The king thought it would be pretty cheap. Who was right - the king or the architect? (there are 64 squares on a chessboard. If you double every time just on the first half of the board, you'd have 4 billion dollars... work out what the second half of the chessboard is worth - it's a lot more than that! If you have a real chessboard, you can actually play putting pennies on the squares until you can't stack enough pennies on a square; it happens more quickly than you'd think. Welcome to the concept of compounding and of exponential growth!).

FUN ACTIVITY - KIDS' YARD SALE

Let your kids, perhaps with some of their friends, have a yard sale. They probably have old clothes, toys, games, books, electronic stuff, or sports kit that they'd like to dispose of. Help them plan - for instance, how to advertise, the need to get enough small change for a 'float,' how to price, and how to bargain.

This could be their first entrepreneurial activity. It may also be time to talk a bit about the values of sustainability and reducing waste.
Be receptive if they want to talk about why they are selling things. There may be some lessons there about impulse buying or peer pressure, but it's best to let them think through the subject themselves.

Just prompt, "wow! You're selling that? two years ago, you really really wanted it. What changed?"

FUN ACTIVITIES OUT AND ABOUT

FUN ACTIVITY – COMPARISON SHOPPING

Teach them about comparison shopping when out and about at the store. One week buy an own brand, the next a known brand and teach them how you choose between the two brands and the price difference. Discuss if they think it is worth spending the extra money on the well-known brand.

TEENAGERS

BY THE TIME YOUR KIDS ARE TEENAGERS, THEY SHOULD BE pretty money savvy. However, they won't necessarily have all the tools they need in terms of doing the actual calculations for loans.

WHAT YOUR KIDS KNOW AT THIS AGE

They probably spend a large amount of their time on social media. So they see a constant show-reel of friends, family and celebrities, and it's often focused on consumer goods, branding, what everyone else owns or aspires to. So you may hear a lot of "Mom, Josh's dad bought him a brand-new car for his 18th birthday. Why do I have to drive this old wreck?" or "Mom, this girl at school hired out a whole theme park for her 16th birthday. Can I do that too?"

It's important that your kids learn about contentment. Perhaps that takes us away from pure financial education and into the realms of philosophy, but they should know that they can find happiness without needing to have the most fashionable brand, to have been to the 'in' destination on vacation, or to have the latest videogame. Remember, contentment starts from the heart so show them this - and yes, you can sympathize with their desires, even while you're telling them there are other things in life.

Aspirations get bigger as children get older, and they will often start to have big ideas about their future. This typically means they want more costly things – holidays with their friends, the latest cool gadget, new experiences, wanting to drive and maybe have their own car. But they'll also need to think about how they're going to pay for those big dreams. So this may be a good time to start talking about your own financial life - where you started, how you progressed, what you decided to prioritize and what, perhaps, you decided wasn't so important. Don't moralize - keep it real.

$ "My time at law school, I worked in a bar to pay my way, I practically lived on Pot Noodles, and I think in between the job and studying, I got about six hours' sleep and no time for any fun. I'm glad I did it, but I'm also glad I moved from corporate law to working for the Disability Rights Network. I make less money, but I make a real difference to people's lives."

$ "The worst thing was taking on my first employee. Suddenly, I was responsible for someone else. Some months after I'd paid them, I had no money left for myself! But it was worth the stress. You can see we're not living hand-to-mouth now!"

$ "I never took a degree and that's been a bit of a limitation for me. Last year, I missed out on a promotion that would have paid for a new car and given me a much more interesting job. So... well, that's history. Now I have you guys!"

$ "You know I find the budget really tight some months. When you were tiny, I had to manage one meal a day some months. But at least we don't have to worry about having a roof over our heads because now I've paid off the home loan. For me, just not having to worry about that is a big thing."

It's tempting to tell your kids they should do better than you - but don't. Their priorities may be different. By talking about your life, what you're doing is showing them an example - giving them more information about the world. It's good at this stage if you can provide them with access to other sources of information about financial life. That might be on the internet, through friends who are willing to talk about financial issues, or through professionals you know, such as financial planners, brokers, or bankers.

You can give them some really valuable lessons at this age about how to be money savvy. They will learn a lot from you, so set good examples, but you need to give them much more financial responsibility. They may even now have their first real job; you can help them manage their first wage by thinking about how they want to structure the spend/save/give percentages, just like they did with the money jar.

Kids who have their first job suddenly have much more money in their account. That can go to their heads - they feel like 'kings of the world.' So you may need to help keep their feet on the ground, reminding them that money is not an unlimited resource and that it needs to be actively managed and budgeted. If they want to save up for a car or to backpack around the world, it's time for them to work on a business plan.

Yes, it's a big worry when your little baby suddenly has several thousand bucks in a bank account! Will they blow it? Will they end up maxing out the credit card? However, if you've done your job right, you shouldn't need to worry too much. Plenty of studies have shown that children who are given responsibility for certain expenses are more likely to budget and keep track of their money.

Before they apply to college, at some point, you will need to sit down with them and talk to them about how they will pay for it, as it is unlikely you will be paying for it all. It's also good for them to have some responsibility towards paying for their education. Let them know that a student loan would be a last resort and discuss the alternatives with them – going to a community college or an in-state university, getting a part-time job and applying for a scholarship as soon as possible, well in advance of college. You might also stress that their degree, whether it's intended to make money (like a business or law degree) or to fulfill other ambitions (like an arts or drama major), is an investment in themselves. You can, again, draw up a business plan. That might be strictly financial (working on graduate first job salaries, which are available on the internet), or it might be more fluid - perhaps setting out several objectives which your youngster wants to achieve.

ALLOWANCES

Giving a teenager a regular allowance gives them the opportunity to practice good money management. They can still help with chores around the house in exchange for their allowance or earn extra by doing specific chores. They're now old enough to do chores for the neighbors, too, such as lawn mowing or car cleaning.

They may even have a part-time job. Or they could start a small business, selling things on online platforms such as eBay or Etsy. For kids with a creative spirit, Etsy can be a great storefront. Make sure they find some good resources to help them plan the business - if you don't have that expertise, find some online resource or a friend who can help.

If your kid is going shopping with friends, give them cash or a prepaid card, not a credit card. If, when they get to the till, they suddenly realize their items total more than the $50 you gave them, they will have learned two lessons. First, to always know exactly what you're spending; secondly, they have to sometimes make tough choices quickly (a famous study out of MIT showed that people will spend twice as much money on the same item when they pay with credit cards instead of cash. While plastic can seem like play money, cash feels all too real).

BUDGETING

You've already started getting your kids used to managing their money, but it's important that they learn how to budget correctly at this age. If you talk to them about your financial responsibilities and how you budget for the things that need to be paid for in life and the things you want, it will help. Tell them about the things you need that you have to pay for; the home bills, the grocery shop, car insurance, gas, plus anything you spend on them, such as school trips or lunches. Tell them about any tips you have for making better use of money, such as an automatic 'sweep' from your current account into your savings account or regular investment plans.

You can also discuss how, for instance, it's cheaper to stock up tinned and frozen goods, toilet paper, and so on by buying two- or three-months supply at once, at bulk prices, rather than buying only when you need. But to be able to do that, of course, you need to have enough money in the bank account to pay for three months' shopping.

There are many different ways they can budget – help them find a budgeting app they can use on their phone. This makes budgeting - which can be a pretty dry topic - a bit more fun by setting goals and tracking progress. EveryDollar is a simple budgeting app they can use which has a free or premium version. Many new generation banks can also help with budgeting apps and even let customers divide their savings into different 'jars' ('holiday,' 'car,' 'regular expenses,' 'college') - just as you did with coins when your kids were much younger.

It is important to set boundaries with the money you give them. The people who have the most problems managing money in later life are often those who could always depend on their parents to bail them out when they got into trouble. It is much better if your kids learn their lessons now with a few hundred bucks rather than with thousands of dollars later on!

SETTING THE RIGHT EXAMPLE

Kids look up to their parents, and so it is important that you practice what you preach. They're more likely to copy if they see you saving for something. But if you're quick to turn to your credit cards to buy something and always flinch when the bank statement arrives, they'll learn your bad habits instead.

If you do need to do something that may be against your normal principles because of short-term financial pressures, for instance, just be honest with your kids and explain to them why you're making that choice in this situation. It's not unknown for teenagers who are earning their own money to offer to help out if their parents are finding the situation tough; a sign that they really are becoming an adult.

If you've made financial mistakes, be honest and admit it. For instance, if you've ever maxed out your credit cards, why was that? It's obviously a different story if you did so to set up your own business (but talk about the risk) rather than to pay for spring break in Cancun. Likewise, if you had a tough time repaying debt, or were ever foreclosed on a house, tell them. Tell them, too, about the house you wish you'd bought, or the jobs you wish you'd taken - why you took certain decisions and whether you'd necessarily do the same thing again.

Be prepared for all the marketing that will hit them as soon as they turn eighteen and help them to keep their feet on the ground. Credit card companies will be trying to sell them 0% credit offers, huge credit limits, all kinds of stuff, so it's not surprising that debt becomes a huge problem for many young adults. Talk about the different types of debt and explain which are more expensive and which are less expensive over the long term.

HELP THEM FIGURE OUT HOW TO MAKE MONEY

Teenagers have plenty of free time and will usually spend this hanging out with friends, scrawling through social media, playing video games, or whatever else they enjoy doing. They have long breaks from school

– fall, summer, winter, spring breaks. During these breaks, they might find a job or become a small-scale entrepreneur.

Getting a job brings with it a new level of financial understanding and you can help them build on this. Go through their first payslip to explain the various deductions - the concept of tax comes as a nasty surprise to some teenagers. It's particularly important that they understand the difference between gross and net pay - a $75,000 salary doesn't mean you have $75,000 coming into the bank!

There are a lot of young entrepreneurs out there and they often start small, selling unwanted stuff on eBay or selling to the local neighborhood. Encourage this and help them find inventive ways they can start making some money.

Buy the Teen entrepreneur toolbox to help them get started. This is a bestselling guide to help teens who are just beginning their entrepreneurial journey. It's particularly useful if you yourself have never run a small business because if you don't have all the answers, the toolbox does.

INVESTING

So far, you've taught your kids to save. But now it's time to teach them a bit about investing. You may need to do a bit of learning new stuff yourself if this isn't an area you know much about - but you only need to stay one step ahead, at first. If your kids really get interested, they'll be able to find loads of resources on the internet - and teach you a bit about the market! Discover it together - that can be even more fun!

Talk about how banks work; they take deposits (the money you have in your bank account) and they then lend out the money to make interest. Why do your children think borrowers pay higher interest rates than savers? That's how the bank makes its money. Talk about protection (the Federal Deposit Insurance Corporation in the US, or Financial Services Compensation Scheme in the UK). Regulation is boring, but make sure they know that they should check out banks and brokers are members of the right associations and registered properly with the regulator.

It's time now to introduce kids to the stock market. Start when they are about twelve or so by playing stock market games or making a 'fantasy' portfolio. Talk about the fact that by investing in a productive enterprise - whether through the stock market or in their own business - they are helping to create wealth. Buying stocks isn't a kind of gambling; it's investing in a business like Coca-Cola, Microsoft, or Ford Motors. Suggest that they might look up different approaches to investing - for those who are a bit nerdy, exploring the Investopedia website can be fun.

Talk about the difference between direct investing and investing through funds. It's important they know about the costs of different types of investment and the costs of going through a financial advisor rather than running their own portfolio. Fees can take a huge slice of their wealth over the long term - yes, it's the effect of compounding, again.

You might also want to talk about booms and busts and address the appeal of 'story stocks' and the glamour of the stock market and day trading against long-term investment, which some people find a bit more tedious. Suggest they Google names like Benjamin Graham,

Warren Buffett, and Peter Lynch. If you're not an expert, there are quite a few sites where youngsters can find information, like stockmarketgame.org or howthemarketworks.com.

SAVING

Once your teenager gets a job, this gives them much more available cash. Before the money starts to come in, ask them how they plan to divide up their wage. They may want to save for their first car or for college. If you use a standing order/banker's order to move money into a savings or investment account each month, show them how it works and help them set up a similar arrangement for themselves.

If they don't have a bank account yet, help them set one up. This will take money management to the next level and will prepare them for managing a much heftier account when they're older.

You might want to set up a monthly review. Did they get their regular expenses budget right? How much cash were they left with at the end of the month? What do they want to do with it? Make it into a business-like presentation and remember to allow them their independence - though you can still point out the possible problems with certain decisions. You might also point out that "I'm going to spend it all on a good night out" is a decision that might work if they're spending what's left of their wage after all their expenses have been paid and they've made a $200 transfer to their savings account - but not otherwise!

In the UK, your kid may have a junior ISA. Unfortunately, there are no equivalent tax-exempt accounts in the US. Show them how much can be paid in, in addition to the current balance. Ask them to think of companies they'd like to invest in and then research together which ones may be a good investment. This helps them learn how the stock market works and the importance of spreading money across different investments.

Keep reminding them of the magic of compounding, whether that's compounded interest or reinvested dividends from their shares. The earlier you can get them investing, the better because they will take what they learn into adult life. It'll give them a head start in preparing for their future. And, of course, if they start investing in their 20s, they'll end up with far more wealth when they get older.

RISK

Many programs for teaching children about finance miss this out, but an educated approach to risk is one of the most important things you can teach them.

Sometimes it's right to run a risk. Starting your own business is always a risk, but sometimes it's right to take that risk. For example, investing in stocks rather than keeping money in the bank has higher risk but also delivers higher rewards. Ask your children how they'd work out whether to take a risk or not and what they might want to check out before they do so.

You might also talk about balancing risks with your financial circumstances - for instance, if you are making good money and own your home, you can afford to buy higher-risk shares; if you are renting and have an insecure job, you'd want to be more conservative.

FUN ACTIVITIES AT HOME

FUN ACTIVITY - LET THEM RUN THE HOUSE

Let them take over your budget for one week. At the end of the week, ask them how they felt about it? Did they have any challenges? Was it harder than they first expected? What valuable lessons did they learn? Were there aspects of the job that they found more challenging than others? Or that they didn't realize they needed to budget for?

FUN ACTIVITY - START A BUSINESS

Sit down and think whether they could do something to create a small business. For instance, some kids could write an app - maybe a game, or perhaps a niche app that helps with particular tasks. Others might make quilts or want to tackle the challenge of upcycling small furniture they find at local thrift stores. Even selling unwanted items on eBay is a good start; you might want to help them work out how much that might make.

If the business works, then you might want to talk about having a budget for the business. That might include investing in a website or buying some books on entrepreneurship.

FUN ACTIVITY - INTERVIEW GRANDPARENTS

Get the grandparents (and other relatives and friends if you can) involved. Get your kids to interview them about money. Do they wish they had saved more into their pensions? How did they save money when they were younger? What was the biggest financial purchase they ever made and how did they pay for it? What was the biggest risk they ever took? What has been their biggest lesson about money? What do they wish they had known earlier about money? If they could go back, are there any money habits they'd change?

It's really good if you then help your kids to produce a little newspaper with the interviews they've done. Then, they can post it as part of their Christmas card!

FUN ACTIVITY - RETIREMENT SAVINGS

Teach them about the importance of saving for retirement from a young age. Then, show them different ways they could do that, including, of course, pensions. There are many pension calculators online; let them play around with monthly payments to see what it would build up to by the time they retire. A particularly interesting thing to do is to start those payments at twenty, at thirty, or at forty, and see how the earlier you start saving, the more you get compared to what you put in.

You might also talk about other ways of creating wealth that can sustain them in retirement. For instance, if they own a business, could they sell it before retirement? Owning real estate might be a way to finance their retirement or having a large investment portfolio that pays dividends. What are the risks of doing that?

You might even introduce your kids to the FIRE movement - Financial Independence, Retire Early. That will introduce them to a lot of interesting financial thinking. It's fair to say, though, not everyone wants to run their lives the FIRE way.

FUN ACTIVITY – BATTLE OF THE STOCKS

Sit down as a family and each pick a stock. If you have younger children, they can join in too, though they may not understand very much about what you're doing. Every week, compare your share prices and don't forget to check if the stock paid a dividend. Chart your progress on the wall. Who's got the most at the end of the year?

You might have started just buying stocks whose names you knew (like MacDonald's or Coca-Cola or Walmart), but as the competition progresses, you'll find out more and more about them. For added fun, pick a stock at random from the financial pages of a newspaper or a screen of the S&P 500 or FTSE 100 stocks. If the random stock wins, you all lose!

FUN ACTIVITY - FANTASY PORTFOLIO

Older teenagers will find this a rewarding step into the stock market. If you get a magazine or report from your broker or from a fund manager, that's useful material for starting off. Then, ask your youngster to put together a portfolio of ten to twenty stocks and follow the portfolio together on a site like zacks.com or advfn.co.uk.

Ask them to put together a presentation for the family on why they invested in these stocks. Then ask for a six-month review. How did they do?

FUN ACTIVITY - AROUND THE WORLD IN 20 STOCKS

Most investors focus on their domestic market. But it might be fun to travel to the UK, France, Germany, Switzerland, India, South Korea, Japan, Taiwan, China... maybe even to African or Latin American stock exchanges and find out what are the biggest stocks on their markets. Then find out a bit about the companies.

FUN ACTIVITY - THE BERKSHIRE HATHAWAY ANNUAL REPORT

Most annual reports are really dull. But Warren Buffett and Charlie Munger have always told it like it is, and the letter to shareholders in the annual report is well worth reading. They talk about the economy at large as well as about their investments and 'the sage of Omaha' has a nice homey, wise-grandad approach. This is one for the junior finance nerd - but it can be fun for you to read together, as well. And you will find a lot of adult investors who make this the one annual report that they read every year.

HELPING YOUR ADULT CHILDREN

YOU DON'T NEED TO STOP TALKING TO YOUR CHILDREN about money once they reach adulthood. If you've done your job right, they will want to come to you to talk through their big decisions - first car, first home, first sabbatical, first career change... as well as perhaps a first child of their own!

But they will only do that if, throughout their childhood, you've shown them that money is something that they can talk about openly with you and that you are not going to be judgmental about their decisions. So as long as they have talked things through, and you are open and honest with them, then if they decide to invest all their savings in setting up an alpaca ranch or a nanotechnology Marketplace, that's fine (tip; ask them about their exit route).

If they have money worries, let them know that you will help them think things through. If they're taking a big risk and you think they have really thought it through, you might decide to offer a guarantee or a bail-out - or an equity investment in the business - but don't get into the habit of helping out every six months. Make sure, if you do lend them money or invest in the business, you get proper legal documents drawn up and treat it as an arm's length transaction.

Remember, too, that everyone, in the end, develops their own financial strategies and objectives. Your children may not attach the same importance as you to owning a home, for instance, or they may decide they'd rather work in start-ups (with all the risks involved) than go work in a major legal firm. Of course, you need to respect that. But if you've done your work right, you have given them the toolbox they need to think through their decisions properly.

You'll also have ensured that they know how to resist temptations - even if they sometimes decide not to - and how not to be scammed. And most of all, you will have helped them grow up into young adults who don't have a complex about money. As a result, they won't feel guilty about having money, they won't feel low self-esteem if they earn less than their friends and they won't screw up their finances by being unable to control their spending.

Better still, when they get together with a partner, they'll be able to talk calmly and sensibly about how the financial side of their future together is going to work. And if they have children, they'll know just how to teach them about money.

AFTERWORD

MONEY IS A FRAUGHT SUBJECT IN MANY FAMILIES. I KNOW IT was in mine. Too little (or too much) money, fear of opening bank statements, spendthrift tendencies, jealousy, envy, despondency; it's a very emotional subject.

So one big thing you can do for your kids is to speak about money calmly, reasonably, and without any sense of it being a taboo subject.

Openness makes such a huge difference; let me tell you a story to illustrate that.

One of my friends spent months telling her kids that everything was fine, when it wasn't. She'd lost her job and taken another job that paid less, and the family budget was very stretched. One day, she broke down in tears and had to tell her kids she was worried about losing their home. Imagine how they must have felt. If, instead, she'd told them about the new job and asked for their help in thinking of ways the family could save money, they would have had a very different feeling about the situation. As it was, she very nearly lost their trust, as they felt she had been lying to them about money.

That's why just talking is so important. Of course you have feelings about money, but you can talk about those quite reasonably. For instance, you can ask your kids "How did you feel when you didn't have any money left that week?", or "Does earning money make you feel better than being given it? Or different?"

Maybe you've had to address some of your prejudices or beliefs about money while you were reading this book. Maybe you're going to need to get educated about banking and the stock market before you can teach your children about how things work. You may not feel terribly confident about your knowledge of money.

But that's fine. At least you've identified areas where you need to put some work in! It's quite likely that some of your issues go back to your parents not having taught you about finance. Now, you can do a better job of parenting your own children, at least when it comes to money.

Remember, too, that you have all kinds of allies you can use, particularly as your kids get older. It's okay for you not to know much about the stock market, but if an uncle or a friend or grandparent knows about investment, ask them to help educate your children. If a friend works in a bank, ask them to talk to your kids about the decisions they have to make. For instance, if they approve loans, they can talk about credit scoring and about how much debt is too much.

You're not trying to bring up mini-tycoons or infant entrepreneurs. Maybe your kids are just going to be regular types. Maybe one of your children is going to decide money isn't important and go off to live in a commune making art and building an off-grid life. Or maybe your fifteen-year-old will create a fantastic app for smartphones and end up selling it for a cool million. Who knows? Your job is to make sure whatever they do, they can handle the financial side of it.

After all, if your entrepreneurial kid got the million bucks and just decided to spend it all, you'd feel that was a poor decision. If they decided to put half of it in investments, most of the rest in the bank, and donate a tenth of the money to a charity they support, you'd feel you had done a great job of bringing them up responsibly. Managing money is a job for rich people as well!

And if your commune-living, pottery-making child ends up managing the commune finances and helping low-income families build their own houses, you could be proud of that, too.

Of course, you want to remember that this is just part of parenting. Make sure your kids know that you love them whether or not they get rich; that you love them even when they make silly decisions, lose money, buy things that aren't worth it, make bad investments, haven't got the patience to save. Love comes first; money comes second.

But it's worth thinking about the way money so often breaks families apart. Often that's because parents haven't talked about money - for instance, what they want to happen to family wealth after they die, or because they bail out a spendthrift senior all the time while the younger sibling makes their own way and feels frustrated and uncared for.

But teach your children right about finance and you'll bring the whole family together. And that can be one of the most powerful things you can do for your kids.

REFERENCES

https://www.forbes.com/advisor/personal-finance/how-to-teach-your-kids-good-money-habits/

https://www.morganstanley.com/wealth/wealthplanning/pdfs/talktokidsaboutmoney.pdf

https://www.moneyhelper.org.uk/en/family-and-care/talk-money/how-to-talk-to-your-children-about-money

https://www.thetimes.co.uk/money-mentor/article/home-schooling-teach-kids-money/

https://www.ramseysolutions.com/relationships/how-to-teach-kids-about-money

https://www.parents.com/parenting/money/family-finances/teaching-kids-about-money-an-age-by-age-guide/

https://www.wired.com/story/how-to-teach-your-kids-about-money

https://www.pbs.org/newshour/economy/making-sense/money-habits-are-set-by-age-7-teach-your-kids-the-value-of-a-dollar-now

https://mascdn.azureedge.net/cms/the-money-advice-service-habit-formation-and-learning-in-young-children-may2013.pdf

https://www.investopedia.com/articles/pf/07/childinvestor.asp

https://www.thebalance.com/top-tips-to-teach-your-kids-about-investing-4115938

https://www.kiplinger.com/investing/602791/7-steps-to-teach-kids-how-to-invest

www.ingramcontent.com/pod-product-compliance
Lightning Source LLC
Chambersburg PA
CBHW051800200326

41597CB00025B/4627